THE
GLOBAL
ENTREPRENEUR

THE
GLOBAL
ENTREPRENEUR

Mary Ayisi

authorHOUSE®

AuthorHouse™ UK Ltd.
1663 Liberty Drive
Bloomington, IN 47403 USA
www.authorhouse.co.uk
Phone: 0800.197.4150

Published by AuthorHouse   11/15/2013

ISBN: 978-1-4918-8369-3 (sc)
ISBN: 978-1-4918-8371-6 (e)

Table of Contents

PREFACE

After the global credit crunch, we all realized how connected the international communities have become. So if you are starting a new business, it is very imperative that you have the globe in mind and do it right first time. This book is a step-by-step guide for setting up and managing a new business. It will motivate and guide you in starting a new or managing an existing business.

This book is for students, graduates, those new to the job market and anyone who is passionate about running their own business to think, plan and go global should their organisation pick up.

To find out more about how to find your passion; how to plan and start the business; how to prepare your own business plan; how to prepare an invoice, how to finance your business, then this book is for you. I have also included about 150 sample business ideas so people who do not have anything yet in mind can build upon that.

INTRODUCTION

Certain realities of the current economy hit me recently as I learnt more about the mentality of many people towards employment.

I am a professional banker working with some of the UK's leading Investment banks. With my banking background and the opportunities offered me in the banking industry, friends and colleagues have sought my advice on many issues, especially about working in the industry.

What recently hit me was that since 2007, the global job market has been struggling, and there has been a significant drop in recruitment and employment of graduates, making the prospects for those taking their first steps on the career ladder look bleak. Because I'm a fan of entrepreneurship, the advice I always give at the end of every conversation with graduates is to be realistic and set up their own businesses. We, as graduates, have to be creative and do make our children's future brighter by putting structures in place for their employment. We have to think of creating employment in our businesses rather than looking for jobs–of becoming employers rather than employees.

When you seek employment, you compete with a number of people for the same job, but when you become an entrepreneur, you rely only on your brainpower and guts as you step into the unknown. Most universities groom students, including the very brainy ones, to be employees rather than employers; as such, your competition as an entrepreneur is already reduced.

In UK and the rest of the world, fewer large national employers are seeking recent graduates than in the past. However, more small and medium-sized enterprises are using the services of university career offices to find new employees. The global financial crisis has impacted different employment sectors very differently, with declines in the number of vacancies being advertised by firms in banking, finance, law, and construction and increases in hiring in the public sector, social care, education, and engineering.

Therefore, anyone with an objective, vision, talent, ideas, and the drive to start a new business and the ability to research a business's competition and potential customers in order to know a business idea's strengths, weaknesses, and opportunities in the market is in a good position. If a person has also developed a clear business plan and is able to put ideas into action, success is certain.

REFLECTION

Richard Lowden, the founder of Eurodrive Car Rental, once said that every time something happens to him, whether positive or negative, he asks himself where the opportunity might be. For example, when people lose their jobs, their first feeling is fear, and little do they think that this event could be an opportunity for them to analyse their employment situations. Chasing after new employment may not be for them, but they will need to do a self-analysis to realise that and their potential for something else. Irrespective of their lifestyles and busy schedules, some people can take time out while they're working to take stock of their lives and learn where they are and where they're going. Unfortunately, other people are unable to do so, and for such people, redundancy could be the best thing that could happen to them, as it will force them to take stock.

Alex McMillan, who started his recruitment business in 1990, was requested by his staff to produce a list of questions to ask new candidates. One of these questions was, If you could get any job in the world and the necessary qualifications, skills, and experience for it, what job would you want? McMillan's firm interviewed 1,000 people, and out of these, 912 of them said they would want to run their own businesses. This goes to show how much people value building a business, and any government should encourage entrepreneurship to secure the future of the economy. Unfortunately, most people are fearful of failure and the uncertainty inherent in setting up and running a business, and they allow that fear to stop them from becoming incredibly successful, realising their full potential, and feeling completely free.

Most people find a job and then go along a conveyor belt until they receive their pensions. They work only for money, not because they're greedy but because they want to be financially secure.

This book is not being targeted at people who want to work only for money and ride the employment conveyor belt. It is for those who want to make a real difference for themselves and to create, excel, achieve, grow, learn, develop, produce, win, accumulate wealth, and make a big impact on their economy. If the latter description fits you, then please read on.

CHAPTER 1

ENTREPRENEURSHIP DEFINED

Entrepreneurs are people who set up business ventures using their own ideas. They take on the risks that come with the business with the intention of increasing the productivity of economic resources, money, labour and raw materials to increase yield.

Entrepreneurs are responsible for leading their firms and demonstrating leadership by choosing competent managerial staff to help run their businesses.

Entrepreneurs have different motives for starting businesses. One is to make money and create wealth, another is to innovate, using money to make their innovative ideas a reality and thereby make more money. Others also start new businesses to meet a need in the market and improve the world in some small way. Some entrepreneurs start businesses for a combination of both of these reasons, and many have entirely different reasons. To be an entrepreneur is to do your own thinking and making your own decisions–thus, you have to be responsible and trust your own judgement.

Two types of people become entrepreneurs:

1. People who identify new commercial opportunities around them by being creative, innovative, and having foresight.

2. Practical people who see and exploit existing opportunities in order to successfully make money.

This is true for owners of small and medium-sized businesses, including the self-employed, artisans, investors, inventors, authors, songwriters, and software developers.

I am of the belief that there are plenty of people out there who dream of starting a new business and have lots of ideas with the potential of Facebook, LinkedIn, Virgin Group, Google, and eBay, but they are not operating today because they fear failing. The saddest thing is that most people have entrepreneurial talent but are not using it and will never use it. These people could be millionaires before they reach the age of thirty. This book is for all those potential entrepreneurs out there: those with the talent, ideas, and drive, and those who are already in business but need to expand or venture into a new field or market to become financially free. I hope this book will release your talent and take you forwards in your journey to establishing and growing a business.

CHAPTER 2

WHY THINK GLOBALLY?

Many people have difficulty thinking with a global mindset and realizing that when something happens in one part of the world, within few seconds, it spreads through other parts of the world. This is how related economies have become.

Businesses have to look internationally for new product ideas, new business opportunities, and growth. When you introduce your product to the international market, your customer base will increase and so will your sales and revenues.

Doing business internationally often requires you to spend a significant amount of time abroad, but as a citizen of the world, you should take full opportunity of the benefits. International travel gives you fresh ideas. As Richard Branson said in his article: (CLASS OF 2013: You'll Never Again Be So Unburdened: Do Something Right) "I would urge you to travel, take on new experiences and draw upon those when it comes to making the decisions that will shape your future. The amount of business ideas that people pick up from travelling the world is enormous. If you don't want to reinvent the wheel, you may find a business that works in another market that could be adapted for your own. Gap years don't only have to happen before you go to college. You might want to take holidays abroad to broaden your mind and look for opportunities".

CHAPTER 3

FINDING YOUR PASSION

Maybe you're unsure where to start. Though most people will have a fairly strong idea of what they want to do, some people will not, probably because they have only just begun to consider entrepreneurship and have yet to think of what business to undertake, how to plan for that business, and when to start it.

To those people who are new to the idea of entrepreneurship, I will start by quoting Benjamin Disraeli, a nineteenth-century British prime minister. He once said that "Man is only great when he acts from passion." This means that you will become successful when you do things you like doing best, when you act out of passion. The best way to finding your passion is to explore avenues of creativity, as these are likely to be the quickest routes to increasing your chances of launching a successful business.

So, you may ask, what are these avenues of creativity?

First, revisit your childhood. Think about what you liked and did best. It is amazing how we become disconnected from the things that brought us joy in childhood. These are the things you should revisit as you reflect on our current situation. Let's say you loved doing the ironing. This means that in your current life, you might enjoy operating a dry-cleaning business. If you loved cooking, you may want to start a restaurant. Perhaps you used to gather other kids around and play teacher. This could mean that you could become a mentor or a teacher by setting up your own private school, after-school club, or breakfast club. American architect Frank Lloyd Wright loved playing with wooden blocks as a child, so it was no surprise that he became an architect.

Second, make a creativity board. In the middle of the board, write "New Business", and create a collage of images, sayings, articles, poems, and other sources of inspiration. When you surround yourself with images of your intention for who you want to become or what you want to create, your awareness and passion will grow and will help you to think big. As your board evolves and becomes more focused, you will begin to recognise what is missing, and you'll imagine ways to fill the blanks and realise your vision.

You can also make a list of people who are doing what you want to do. All you have to do is to study the people who have achieved success in the field you're interested in. For example, you may want to be in the real estate market; however, this industry was badly hit by the current recession, and many businesses failed. If real estate is really your passion, don't give up, and study those in the same industry who made it and learn from their strategies.

Next, start doing what you love even without a business plan and even if you haven't yet figured out how to make money from it. Test out what it might be like to work in an area you are passionate about, build your business network, and ask for feedback that will help you eventually develop and refine a business plan. Approaching entrepreneurship this way will show you the value you bring to the market, and testimonials from your colleagues or clients will help you launch the new business. Most importantly, doing it this way will help you conquer your fear of starting a new venture, and the joy of accomplishment will further fuel your creativity.

Finally, take a break from thinking about business. Indulge yourself in creative writing or painting. A day's trip to museums and arts centre or even to the market could give you lots of ideas. All that you have to do on your return is to reflect on what you saw, and the ideas will flow.

CHAPTER 4

GETTING YOURSELF A VISION

As an aspiring entrepreneur, you have to be clear about what you are trying to achieve and where you see yourself in a year, two years, three years, or even five or ten years, because if you don't know where you're going, the chances are that you'll never get there.

Case Study

Gloria wanted to set up an off-licence business to indulge her passion for wine. After reviewing the numbers, it became clear that one off-licence was not enough to pay her bills, and to do so, she would have to spend every hour of every day working on her business, meaning that she would have no time for her family and friends.

So, Gloria went back to the drawing board and came up with a plan to open three off-licences within the next three to five years, each with its own manager. This clear vision gave Gloria the motivation she needed and also meant that she could fit her working hours around her family's schedule. Finally, it became possible for her to put her plans into action and make her idea fly.

Exercise

Analyse the current situation of your finances, work, family, leisure, health, and well-being and your vision for them in the next one, three, five, and even ten years, and write down your ideas in the table below. This can be very tricky but is vital in your quest to unlocking financial freedom.

	Where I am now	Where I want to be	How I will get there
Finances			
Work/Business ideas			
Family			
Leisure			
Health/well-being			

In order to get the ball rolling, write down three things in the final column in order to achieve your goals.

My friends, family and colleagues have told me that people with a clear plan to put into action are more likely to be successful as well as being better off financially than those who don't.

CHAPTER 5

IS MY BUSINESS IDEA UP TO IT?

All businesses need to ask important questions about their customers and competitors to learn important information about them. When you are able to answer these questions, you increase the chances that your business idea is going to work. If you cannot yet answer these questions, don't worry, as you'll find out the answers as you learn more.

Case Study

Angela enjoys working with children, and one day, her best friend advised her to use her talents and abilities to set up her own crèche. Angela carefully researched the area where she wanted to set up the business. She spoke to mothers in the business's potential catchment area to see how many people would need her services, and she found out how many similar services were provided in the area. Her research revealed that the nearest competitor was over eleven miles away, which meant that if she was able to start her crèche, it would be more convenient for the local mothers than the competition. Angela also searched the Internet to get a rough idea of the hourly rate her competitors charged and how much local parents would be comfortable paying. The information Angela learned about her competitors and their pricing and her potential customers gave her confidence that she could start her business straight away.

Exercise

Answer the following questions:

1. What product or service does your business offer?

2. Who are your customers, and what do you know about them? Knowing these details will help you to effectively target them with your products and services.

3. How big is the market you want to attract? Realistically, how many of these customers are you likely to attract?

4. With all the products and services available from your competitors, why should customers buy your products or take advantage of your services? How are they going to buy and when would they buy what you offer?

5. How much do your competitors charge for the same product or service? How much are customers willing to pay? This information will determine how much you can charge.

6. Are your prospective customers willing to buy what you offer? Is demand for your products or services likely to change, and, if it does, what would that mean for your business?

7. Who are your competitors? Sometimes competition comes in forms that are not obvious, so you need to think widely here.

8. Where are your competitors located? What do you know about them?

9. Are your competitors' customers happy with their products and services?

10. Why are your products and services better than your competitors'? You cannot expect your customers to understand this if you, the provider, do not know the answer.

11. What is your unique selling point, your USP? All successful businesses live and breathe their customers. They know who their customers are, why and how they buy, what is important to them, and what price they can afford. So, businesses use this information to their advantage. It's important that you also make sure that you're clear about what your USP is in order to increase sales.

So you can see why the USP is important, let's say you're in a lift with a prospective customer going one floor up, and you only have thirty seconds to sell your products to this person. How are you going to persuade this customer in such a short time? This is called the "elevator pitch". In a nutshell, it answers, why should the customer buy from you and not your competitor?

STRATEGIC ANALYSIS

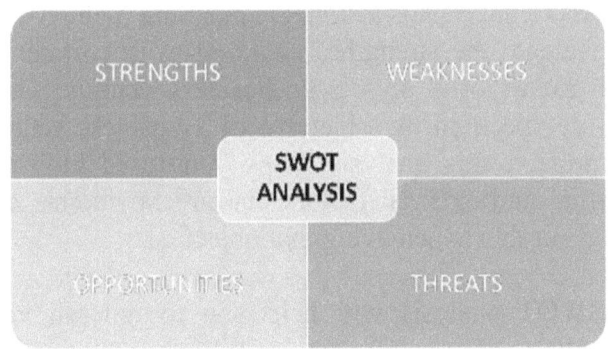

SWOT Analysis

CHAPTER 6

SWOT ANALYSIS

A SWOT analysis is a strategic planning method used to evaluate the strengths, weaknesses, opportunities, and threats of a project or business venture. Once you've specified the objective of a business venture or project, this analysis helps you to identify the internal and external factors that are favourable and unfavourable to achieving that objective.

A SWOT analysis will help you to unleash your potential.

Making a SWOT analysis starts with defining a desired end state or objective. The next step is to analyse its strengths. Your strengths are the characteristics of your business or team that give it an advantage over others in the industry, and your weaknesses are characteristics that place your business or team at a disadvantage.

Your opportunities are the chances outside the business to make greater sales or profits, and the threats are also elements outside the business that could cause it trouble.

Identifying your SWOTs is essential because subsequent steps in planning for the achievement of your objective derive from this analysis.

The SWOT analysis helps you to determine whether your objective is attainable, given the SWOTs. If the objective is *not* attainable, select a different objective and repeat the analysis.

To start a business, you have to analyse how well you know yourself to learn what your strength and weaknesses might be, what you enjoy doing best, and what you would rather not do until later or at all. Being honest with yourself now will save you a lot of pain, money, and inconvenience later.

Case Study

Albert decided to set up his own business as a private marketing consultant, but he also knew he was not good with numbers. He realised that before his business could survive, he needed to keep his accounts in order. Having given the matter some thought, he enrolled in a course at his local college to learn basic bookkeeping.

Then, as his business expanded, he paid for the services of an accountant. This eventually helped him to keep on top of his expenses, to ensure all his suppliers were paid on time, and to keep his bank manager and the taxman happy.

Exercise

Take out a pen and paper and write down the answers to these questions: What are your strengths–what you are really good at doing–and how can you make the most of them? What are your weaknesses, and how can you deal with them? That is, what and how can you improve? What are the opportunities available to you, and how can you make these feature in your business? Also, write down your dislikes and how you can cope with them. Please be really honest with yourself, as running your own business is a big commitment. Many businesses survive their first year, but a lot of them do not. In order to ensure success, being honest with yourself about what exactly you want to do is essential.

Once you have identified your strengths, weaknesses, opportunities, and threats, ask yourself what experience you have that will help you as you embark on your new business and how you could make the most of them or plug the gaps.

CHAPTER 7

THE MARKETING MIX

If you do not win customers, your business will not go far, and after your business is well established, you have to find ways of keeping your customers. This brings us to the marketing mix.

There are seven elements in the marketing mix:

- ❖ Product

- ❖ Price

- ❖ Place

- ❖ Promotion

- ❖ People

- ❖ Physical evidence

- ❖ Process

Product: What kind of product are you offering? What are its features? What are the advantages and benefits of the product?

Price: How much will you charge for your products or services? What payment structures will you adopt, and how much are your competitors charging?

Place: How will you serve your target market? Will you work from home or have premises?

Promotion: How will you promote your business and its products to the target market?

People: Will you employ people or work on your own? What sort of people will work in your business?

Physical evidence: How do you want your business to appear to customers and prospective customers?

Process: What processes should I introduce to meet my business needs and keep customers coming back for more?

CHAPTER 8

AVAILABLE BUSINESS OPPORTUNITIES I HAVE COME UP WITH

Children
Special Occasion yard signs
Personalised or interactive music and story CDs/software
Inflatable party rentals
Personalised books and novelties
Online tutoring and test preparation
Safety products and services
Specialty play equipment sales and events
Fundraising programmes
Toys, software, and games
Gym, art, and sports programmes
Birthday party planning
Day care monitoring and locating service
Movement and fitness education
Child and pet identification system
Music and movement programme
Tutoring referral services
Home tutoring service
Specialty Play Equipment
Preschool fitness programme
Sewing classes
Language education
Tennis and golf lessons
Science education products and services
Custom movies for birthday parties and events
Maths learning system
Playground cleaning service
Children's Bibles
Educational films

Baby handprint/footprint and bronzed keepsakes
Theme parties
Music education
Bicycles
Pre- and post-natal fitness programmes
Cooking programmes
Educational entertainment programmes
Craft and art classes

Internet/Technology
Computer products
Electronic and wireless
Internet consulting
Video games
DVD sales
Website hosting

Finance and Accounting
Accountancy firm
Audit firm
Tax adviser
Financial consultancy

Food
Burgers, fries, and malts
Ice cream shop
Restaurant meal-delivery service
Shaved ice and frozen desserts
Food trailers and carts/Fast Food Franchise
Gourmet foods and gifts
Tea parties
Bulk candy vending machines
Pizza
Fresh-roasted glazed nuts
Doughnuts
Personalised candy bars, bottled water, and mints
Beverage machine rentals, sales, and catering
Fruit and vegetable arrangement design or classes
Dinner-delivery service
Coffee carts or kiosks
Coffee equipment and consulting
Personalised chocolate
Healthy food vending
Corporate catering

Health Care
Home helpers
Rehabilitation
Elder-care services
Doctors' express urgent care clinic
In-home companions for elderly people
Pharmacy shops
Private clinics
Private midwifery

Sports
Fitness clubs
Youth sports leagues
Adult sports leagues
Sports camps
Sports clinics
After-school sports programmes and activities
Sports photography
Sports magazine or website
Swimming pool
Swimming lessons

Fitness and Beauty
Nutritional products
Hair salon
Children's hair care
Hair-care products
Mobile hair salon
Personal trainer

Cleaning and Maintenance
Dry cleaning
Home improvements
Carpet cleaning
Landscaping
Home cleaning service
Coin laundry
Environmental waste solution

Education
After-school programmes
Private school

Business coaching
Employment agency
Learning centres: maths, English, etc.
Event planning/organising
Business advisory
Employee education, coaching, assessments, and consulting

Home Products and Services
Residential and commercial painting
Disaster restoration
Commercial, residential, and auto locksmith

Retail
Sports goods
Children's clothing
Children's products
Computer products
Electronic and wireless products
Food and grocery
Online retail
eBay shop
Auto paint and bodywork
Pets supply
Printing and visual communications
Specialty food and beverage
Tools and hardware
Travel services
Photo booth
Family entertainment
ATM
Gift cards
"Sports Clips": barber shop with giant TVs
UPS franchise

CHAPTER 9

BUSINESS PLAN

A business plan is an operating tool that will guide you to successfully start and run your business. Such a plan helps owners of new or existing businesses take an objective look at their businesses to identify areas of strength and weakness, pinpoint needs that otherwise might be overlooked, spot opportunities early, and plan how to best achieve their goals.

In order for any business to survive, it needs a business plan, as preparing one forces you to take an objective, critical, and unemotional look at your business project as a whole. When you do so, you are able to avoid problems that you may encounter as you run your business.

A business plan will also help banks, venture capital firms, and business angels to evaluate your venture if you seek help from them. It will act as a complete financing proposal, so it allows you to use the same plan regardless of which company you approach.

Most business plans will end up with a bank, so it is imperative that you are aware of how banks view business plans and what questions they ask when they view them, because they take risk into consideration. Whilst it is their wish that a business survives and makes a profit, they also want to ensure that a loan they give you will be repaid. Some of the questions they ask are:

- What is the nature of the business?

- What is the purpose of the loan you seek?

- What is the amount of the loan?

- Does the business have the ability to repay the loan?

- What is the character and management skill of the business owner?

Note that if your business is a new start-up and seeking financing, you might not have the experience and the track record that banks are looking for, but a well-organised, insightful business plan can convince a banker or other funder of your ability to understand your market, demonstrate your technical knowledge in the field, and show the company's ability to understand and respond to customer needs. The plan must ultimately show your ability to manage the business so it can be profitable and repay its loans.

When you write your business plan, the items below are some of the most important areas to include.

Executive Summary

An executive summary is a short document or section of a document produced for business purposes that summarises a longer report or proposal or a group of related reports in such a way that readers can rapidly become acquainted with your business without having to read a large collection of materials. The executive summary will usually contain a brief statement of the problem the business addresses or proposal for the business covered in the rest of the plan, background information about the business, a concise analysis, and main conclusions. This section aids managers in making decisions and could possibly be the most important part of the business plan, for it summarises the key points from which one can make decisions with the business plan. Even though this is the first item on the list, it is usually written last.

Mission Statement

A mission statement is an official statement of the aims and objectives of a business. It is a declaration of what a business aspires to be. It describes the business's reason for being, clarifies of who the business serves, and expresses what it hopes to achieve in the future. A properly written mission statement accurately describes the business and motivates or reassures the people who contribute to its success. This statement helps to answer questions such as the following:

- ❖ What business are we really in?

- ❖ What type of business do we want to be?

- ❖ What is our target market?

- ❖ What inspires us?

The characteristics of a mission statement are:

It is visionary, as it helps people understand what the business is about and how those people can contribute to achieving that vision.

It is broad enough to describe how the company meets the needs of its customers without annual revisions.

It is realistic, which means it is practical and workable. An over-reaching, unrealistic mission statement will not have great credibility. Instead, the best statements are direct and powerful.

And, finally, it is motivational. The mission statement should inspire all stakeholders in the business–its customers, employees, partners, and funding agencies–about what the company will do or produce.

History of Your Business

This provides historical details about the business, including the founding date, major successes, and strategically valuable experiences.

Product or Service

Your product or service should be described here in simple terms so that everybody will understand them. This section should include:

- ❖ What makes it different

- ❖ What benefits it offers

- ❖ Why customers would buy it from you instead of your competitors

- ❖ How you plan to develop it

- ❖ Whether you hold any patents, trademarks, or design registration

- ❖ The key features and success factors of your industry or sector

Remember that you are the one who best understands your business and its product or service and that the person reading the plan might not, so it is important to avoid jargon.

Market Research

You should refer to any market research you have carried out already as you define your market, your position in the market, and who your competitors are. This section demonstrates that you are fully aware of the marketplace you plan to operate in and that you understand any important trends and drivers. You should also be able to demonstrate that even in fierce competition, your business will be able to attract more customers over time.

The key areas to cover in this section include the following information:

- ❖ Your market: its size, historical data about its development, and key current issues

- ❖ Your target customer base: who they are and how you know they will be interested in your products or services

- ❖ Your competitors: who they are, how they operate, and what share of the market they hold

- ❖ The future: changes you anticipate in the market and how you expect your business and your competitors to react to them

It is important to know your competitors' strengths and weaknesses relative to your own, and it is good practice to do analyse each competitor. Remember that the market is not static. Your customers' needs and your competitors can change, so as well as showing your analyses of your competitors, you should also demonstrate that you have considered and drawn up contingency plans for the future.

Marketing Plan

The objectives of the marketing plan for a new product must identify all other substitute products. The plan must explain the name of the substitute, its features, why it is a substitute, and why your proposed product is better than the substitute. You should also detail the switching costs, why a new product justifies switching, expected adoption dynamics, and the expected role once the market begins to develop.

Organisation and Management

This section should introduce the management team, including the names of board members, owners, senior managers, and managing partners.

Operational Details

In this section, you outline your operational capabilities and any plans for improvement. This section should focus on these areas:

- ❖ Location: Does your business operate on a property outside your home? Do you own the property or rent it? What are the advantages and the disadvantages of the location of the business?

- ❖ Producing your goods and services: Do you have your own facilities for production? Will you need any investments for production? Who is going to be your supplier?

❖ Management information system: This is a system for tracking stock, performing quality control, and managing accounts.

❖ Information technology: Information technology is very important in many businesses. You should indicate the strengths and weaknesses of your business's IT in this section and outline any plans for development of that system.

Financial Forecast

This is the section in which you translate all you have said in your business plan to this point into numbers. If you will need financial assistance, state here how much capital you will need and the security you can provide in order to get the assistance. You will also need to state how you plan to repay any borrowings as you confirming your sources of revenue and income. At this stage, you can also include your personal finances.

Your forecasts should run for the next three or even five years, and their level of detail should reflect the sophistication of your business. However, the first twelve months' forecasts should provide the most detail. Include the assumptions behind your projections with your figures, both for costs and revenues, so investors can clearly see the thinking behind the numbers.

This section should include:

- ❖ Sales forecast

- ❖ Cash flow forecast

- ❖ Profit and loss forecast

- ❖ Risk analysis

Objectives and Action Plan

Your business objectives should be SMART: specific, measurable, achievable, realistic, and time-bound.

- ❖ Specific: Give real numbers, not estimates. For example, you might set an objective of getting one hundred new customers.

- ❖ Measurable: Whatever your objective, you need to be able to check whether you have reached it when you review your plan.

- ❖ Achievable: You must have the resources you need to achieve the objective. The key resources are usually people and money.

- ❖ Realistic: Targets should stretch you but not demotivate you because they are unreasonable or out of reach.

❖ Time-bound: Set a deadline for achieving the objective. For example, you might aim to get one hundred new customers within the next twelve months.

CHAPTER 10

BUSINESS AND IT

Information technology (IT) can play an essential role in any business. Once you know the aims of your business, you can see how IT can help you, and can choose the right IT systems to best meet your aims.

With the right IT systems, you can effectively capture, process, store, and use information to improve communication, cut costs, and simplify the way your business runs, thus helping your business grow and find new opportunities.

An IT system involves hardware and software. But how do you choose the right equipment? Start by thinking about how you use a computer in your business, and ask yourself the following questions:

What key jobs do you need to perform? For each job, what data or information do you need? This will give you a basic idea of what equipment you will need.

Will you operate mainly at one place?

Do you need to be mobile?

Will you need to connect to other equipment?

How many computers will you need? One or several linked to a network?

Whatever you choose, make sure it is easy to upgrade as your business grows. Your local computer shop or an online forum will be able to give you specific advice. When you've decided on your equipment needs, you need to decide on whether to buy your hardware outright or lease it from a supplier. Ongoing technical support is also an important consideration to keep everything working as it should.

Whatever you choose, it is important to keep your system secured. That means protecting your data with strong passwords and guarding your systems from external threats such as viruses.

You're then on your way to using the IT system and technical support that is right for you now and in the future plans.

CHAPTER 11

FINANCING YOUR BUSINESS

Assets, Savings, Bonds, and Equity

This form of financing comes out of your own pocket. You can either sell some of your assets or use the savings you've already accrued. This type of finance has its pros and cons, but if you are serious about your business, you'll feel confident that you will not lose the money.

Angel Investors

Angel investors are people who have money that they've made through their own ventures but are looking for opportunities to make more money by earning high returns on the funds they lend. You can locate them by searching the web or attending their seminars and meetings.

Venture Capitalists

Venture capitalists make a lot of small investments. They have industry knowledge, give you ideas, and assist you with marketing, sales, and other operations. There are advantages and disadvantages to obtaining funding from a venture capitalist, and it is up to you to weigh them. One advantage is that they make decisions quickly. However, they will ask for a percentage of your business. If your business is not performing well, they may be able to take over and manage it themselves until they are satisfied with the business's performance. You can find them by speaking to your bankers, searching the web, and attending their seminars and meetings.

Loan from Family Members

When dealing with family, document everything and ensure all parties have a clear understanding of the loan terms. Family members may want a piece of your business, and if you agree to this condition, be sure to stipulate that at your own discretion, you may buy them out in future at a certain price. Another problem with borrowing from family members is that they may be intrusive, perhaps even calling you every day to ask unnecessary questions. However, family members may be more flexible with their terms than other sources and they will be more willing to lend to you than a formal source simply because they know you better than anyone.

Borrowing From Your Bank

Secured loan: This type of loan requires you to put up collateral or a personal guarantee to obtain funds.

- **Micro-loan:** This is a loan in a small amount. You will need a business plan to apply and will also need to show that you cannot obtain conventional financing.

- **Credit card:** This is not the best way to finance a business unless you are financially savvy and can manage this form of borrowing well. The advantage is that you can have access to the money pretty quickly, but interest can also be very high, so it's best to leave this type of financing as a last resort.

- **Overdraft**: A pre-arranged overdraft with your bank could come in handy, as this is a pre-approved credit, so it requires no fresh credit application.

Borrowing from Social Lenders

For this type of financing, people put money into a pool and lend it to you.

Trade Credit

This is credit from your suppliers. They provide you with the goods and services you need with the agreement that you'll pay later.

Crowd Funding

Crowd funding is raising one big lump sum from a large crowd of people, mostly through the internet.

Customers

In some businesses, you can obtain money from customers up front as a deposit and deliver your goods or services later.

CHAPTER 12

FRANCHISE OPTIONS

Franchising is the right to operate using somebody else's business model. Typically, you will pay a franchise fee and ongoing royalties to the franchisor for the right to operate the model for a specified time period.

Franchise agreements typically last from ten to twenty years and, more often than not, come with options to extend the agreement.

In the United States alone, there are over six thousand franchise opportunities available.

Franchises provide an opportunity for a more secure business than others. It is commonly said that most new businesses fail within three years of starting, but most franchise businesses survive longer because the market is already mature. However, you will pay higher start-up costs for choosing a franchise over an independent business because of the fees, royalties, and cost of buying inventory from the franchisor. Also, selling alternative products is not possible in most franchises.

Advantages of Buying a Franchise

Before buying a franchise, consider carefully whether the business model will suit you. If you've found such a franchise, the following advantages and disadvantages are important to consider before buying in.

Advantages:

a. It is your own business.

b. You may avoid many of the problems encountered in the initial years of running an independent business because the franchise's format has already been worked out.

c. You will receive ongoing support and advice.

d. The brand name is already established, and because you'll be paying royalties to the franchisor, you'll receive a huge push in marketing the brand and products.

e. All new franchisees receive training to help them be successful.

f. Although franchisors do not always pass on benefits to franchisees, because of the size of the franchise, the franchisor may have greater negotiating power with suppliers than you would on your own.

Disadvantages:

a. Even though this is your own business, you are not allowed to act on your own. You must always act first in the interest of the franchisor and other franchisees. You may find yourself restricted.

b. You have to pay fees, and part of your profits will have to go to the franchisor each year.

c. The franchisor can demand to see your sales figures at any time and also has the right to enter your premises.

d. You have to adhere to the rules, regulations, and methods laid down by the franchisor, possibly leaving you little room to show your entrepreneurial skills.

e. You may have to purchase all your stock from the franchisor and not be able to shop around for a better deal.

f. If the franchisor's promotions prove ineffective and this affects your business directly, there is little you can do about it unless the contract says otherwise.

g. If you want to sell your franchise before the end of the contract, the franchisor must agree to the sale.

h. If the performance of your franchise is satisfactory and you want to renew the contract after expiry, it could be difficult or impossible to do so. Therefore, you should assess your potential for return within the first years of the contract before investing, because if you are not able to renew, you may have little to sell, and you cannot sell the name and goodwill of the franchise.

Choosing a Franchise

If you've decided to operate a franchise, the following steps will help you be successful:

- Be very sceptical about the franchise, specialists dealing with franchise businesses, and the franchisor. Always choose your own specialist to advise you and do not accept a specialist recommended by the franchisor. Accountants, solicitors, and high-street banks are the best places to find such a specialist, as many have units dealing specifically with franchise businesses.

- Employ an accountant to advise you on the forecast the franchisor gives you, especially how realistic it is.

- Ask your lawyer or solicitor to go through the contract with you carefully, examining every word and all the restrictions.

- Enquire how many franchises have already been sold and how long they have been operating. As you do this, it is best to visit and talk to existing franchisees that you choose yourself. Do not allow the franchisor to pick and choose for you.

- Examine all arrangements for purchasing equipment and stock. You do not want to be pushed into buying new equipment if you don't need it, and you should not enter into an arrangement in which the franchisor can increase the mark-up on the products sold to you. Ask whether it is possible to buy from alternative sources for a fraction of the price or if the franchisor will match the price.

- Ask your franchisor for a copy of the latest financial statements, and send them to your accountant to examine them.

- Research the franchisor. It's highly important that it continues to exist, as it carries all the bargaining power and brand power. You can obtain a reference from a credit rating agency to help you determine its longevity.

- Check whether the franchisor is a member of a franchise organisation in your country or internationally, if it is a global business, as such bodies require their members to abide by a code of conduct.

- Check that the territory where you seek to operate is clearly marked out and that you have a clear map of it. As the franchisor for market research about this territory to determine its potential for sales.

- Do your own market research as if you are starting a new business.

- Find out what will happen if you have a disagreement with the franchisor, you die, or you want to sell or renew your franchise.

- Check that the product you're selling is patented or that its name has been registered, otherwise the franchise you buy could be worthless.

- Find out how advertising is done and maintained. Check to see what plans have been laid down for marketing.

- Assess the franchise in as many ways as you can *before* you commit as a contract, as once you sign, you cannot back out.

The following resources will help you as you do you research:

The UK Franchise Directory http://www.theuk franchisedirectory.net/match/franchises.php?gclid= CPrqzaeQvLcCFbMbtAodxxcA9Q

International Franchise Association

http://www.franchise.org/

Economic Impact of Franchise Businesses

http://www.buildingopportunity.com/download/
National%20Views.pdf

Successful Business

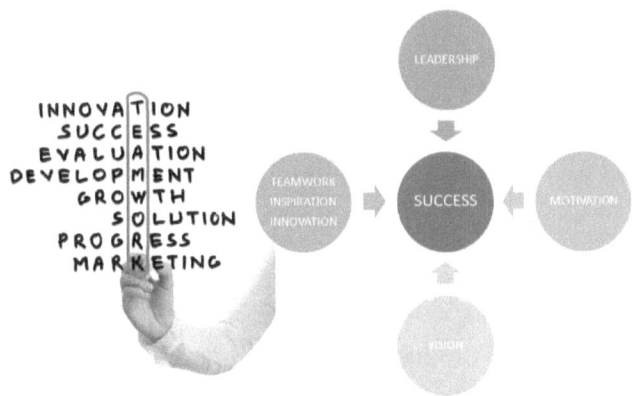

CHAPTER 13

SUCCESSFUL BUSINESSES

This section will give you an understanding of the common pitfalls of running a business. Every year, many new businesses fail, so knowing what might go wrong will give you a greater chance of success.

Case Study

Nick set up his new business selling sports products, but unfortunately, he did not prepare a good cash-flow forecast. His expenses increased whilst he was still struggling to find customers to buy his products, and as a result, his business never got off the ground.

If Nick had produced a proper business plan, he would have known what his initial outlay would have been. This would have helped Nick to put the necessary finances in place to help him whilst he got the business up and running. Whilst Nick's business idea was a good one, he did not plan it properly.

Exercise

Make a list of ten possible reasons your business might fail and what you can to do to counter each one. A business's first year is always the toughest, but the good news is that the vast majority of businesses are still trading after one year. Once they've reached the one-year mark, only a few will fail before they reach the three-year mark.

The following are examples of how your business could slip up and how to avoid each pitfall.

How You Could Fail	Common Mistakes	How To Avoid/Remedy
Wrong target market or not enough customers	- Not doing enough research to locate your customers - Choosing the wrong location - Not understanding the needs of your customers - Not listening to clients - Not understanding your competitors and who they are	- Do proper market research with questionnaires and surveys. - Analyse the results from the survey and use it to form a marketing plan.
Getting your numbers wrong	- Underestimating your costs and not having enough capital - Increase in costs - Delinquent customers	- Overestimate your needs. - Be prepared to tweak your sales and cash flow in the initial stage. - Plan how to deal with delinquent customers.

Financials	- Using short-term funds to buy equipment and supplies (e.g. overdraft) - Relying too heavily on awards and grants - Borrowings from friends and family without clear terms	- Use only long-term funds to purchase long-term products like equipment. - Consider how much you need and then where is best to get it from.
Legislation	- Not following rules such as health and safety - Not getting all your business agreements in writing	- Seek advice from a specialist, such as a lawyer, and have that specialist draw up all the business agreements (e.g. a partnership agreement) for you.
Protecting your idea	- A competitor can duplicate your idea if you do not register your trademark with the authorities	- Always protect your idea by securing the proper intellectual property rights. Seek a specialist assistance.
The taxman	- Missing deadlines for filing taxes - Not having enough money set aside to pay taxes	- Contact Inland Revenue to enquire about the legal requirements regarding taxes. Do not put this aside for later. The economy depends on the taxes you pay, and the survival of your business depends on your paying taxes.

Internet	- Over-designed website which is not user-friendly - No database back-up - Insufficient security to protect business data	- Use tight anti-virus protection to protect your customers' data - Make your website user-friendly. You can do this by hiring a competent web designer. - Make sure that your customers can locate your website easily.
Hiring and firing employees	- Inexperienced candidates/limited skills - Lack of job description - Unclear employment policies	- Use professional employment agencies - Human resources policies changes regularly. Make sure you are up to date with current legislation.
Insurance	- Being underinsured	- Have a contingency plan in place to deal with the what-ifs.

Write down five things that you need to do to prevent these or the pitfalls you came up with from happening. Nobody likes to think about the worst scenario, but it will do you good to understand some of the common mistakes so you can put plans in place for avoiding them.

CHAPTER 14

FINANCIAL REPORTING

Every business needs to keep basic books and accounts for their daily operations. Keeping such books will

- ❖ Show you where you stand financially

- ❖ Help you make financial decisions

- ❖ Help you reduce your tax liabilities and know what your tax liabilities are

- ❖ Correctly collect and pay out VAT

- ❖ Help you during auditing and keep auditing costs down

- ❖ Help you discuss your financial position with others, such as banks

The following are some of the books you need to keep:

Cashbooks

A cashbook is a simple accounting book used to record basic information about cash receipts and payments. The cashbook is available in hard-copy form and also in different types of money management software. This book provides an easy way to keeping up with how much money is coming in and what bills are getting paid and can be effectively used by just about anyone.

Bank Account

Everything you do in business revolves around money. This money needs to be identifiable at every stage of the transaction, and, of course, your business money needs to be separated from your own personal finances. Opening a business bank account is the simplest way to achieve accountability and to provide a good degree of transparency in your business dealings to government departments, creditors, and auditors, allowing them to accurately assess your business. A business account will also give you credibility, as by giving you such an account, your bank has, to a degree, assessed and accepted your business plan.

Balance Sheet

A business's balance sheet shows the financial picture at a specific time, such as at the end of the last day of the month or the end of the last day of the year. The financial picture includes assets, liabilities, and capital. Through the magic of double-entry bookkeeping, your financial transactions can be recorded in a way that ensures the balance sheet will indeed balance if the entries are correct.

Assets are cash, accounts receivable, inventory, land, buildings, vehicles, furniture, and other things the company owns. Liabilities are notes payable, accounts payable, and debts to the bank, suppliers, individuals, and other creditors. Capital is your ownership in the business–stock, investments, and retained earnings.

Profit-and-Loss Account

A profit-and-loss account records sales income, costs, and expenses and shows a business's performance over a specific period of time. A profit-and-loss account also records revenue from sales and the cost of sales plus overhead and expenses to show you whether a profit or loss has been made.

This account also shows a summary of invoices that have been issued, or sales income that has been generated, and an estimate of work in progress that has not yet been invoiced. A profit-and-loss account also includes purchases made from suppliers for goods or raw materials and an estimate of the cost for goods or raw materials the business has used but not yet paid for.

Sales Book

A sales book is a book in which you record details of credit sales made by the business. This book shows the total credit sales of goods during a specified period. Usually, the sales book is totalled every month, but you can do a daily sales record in the daily sales book from copies of invoices sent out.

Invoice

An invoice, also known as a bill, is an itemised list of goods shipped or services rendered, stating quantities, prices, fees, shipping charges, and other charges. Once you've extended credit to your customers, invoicing them on a regular basis becomes your next most important task when it comes to getting paid for your products and services. When invoicing clients, make sure that there is no error in the address or the spelling of their name. Spell out the payment terms, and clearly define the due date for payment. Use electronic invoicing, as handwritten invoices are always prone to mistakes, and for clarity's sake, invoices should be written in terms that everyone understands.

For customers you do business with only occasionally, make sure you spell out the payment terms properly. If you do regular business with a customer, keep a statement of account, a recap of all the invoices sent to that customer during a given month, and send it monthly. This statement should list each invoice by number, date delivered, and amount due.

Be sure to stay organised and know how your system works. Remember that if you don't promptly bill your customers, they have the luxury of using your money interest-free.

Purchase Order

According to Wikipedia, this is "a commercial document … issued by a buyer to a seller indicating the types, quantities, and agreed-upon prices for products or services the seller will provide to the buyer. Sending a purchase order to a supplier constitutes a legal offer to buy products or services. Acceptance of a purchase order by a seller usually forms a [one-off] contract between the buyer and seller, so no contract exists until the purchase order is accepted.[1]

Stock-Record Card

A stock-record card keeps track of inventory. A reliable and efficient inventory-tracking system provides your business with data about quality and timeliness that ultimately improves operational efficiency and also helps in managing products, items, or parts within the business.

Bank Reconciliation

A bank-reconciliation statement shows the items that making up the difference between the balance according to the cash book and the balance on the bank statement.

---

1   "Purchase order", *Wikipedia* < http://en.wikipedia.org/wiki/Purchase_order>, accessed 8 Oct. 2013.

CHAPTER 15

CONCLUSION

Now that you've learned about starting a business, you can determine whether you'd prefer to be an entrepreneur or whether you are happy seeking employment that will take you months if not years to find. If you're already employed, you can assess whether you're happy being an employee making lots of money for other people. If not, are you ready to find out what life would be like if you stepped into the unknown and launched your own business?

If it seems you'd be happier running your own business and if you have faith and can take risks, then start something new. Many businesses don't require a huge amount of start-up capital, allowing you to minimise your risk of losing money.

On the other hand, if you are not yet ready to take such a risk and you don't have faith that you can run a new business full time, then please find or stay in employment. With hard work, you will earn a regular salary, and eventually you may be able to operate your own business in your spare time until you've gained enough confidence to take it on full time.

Whatever you want to do in life, be bold and take a step forward. If you act like an entrepreneur, people will trust you and will want to do business with you. Please note that nobody is born an entrepreneur, but with determination, hard work, and positive endorsements, your ideas will move forward and people will soon see you as an entrepreneur. The following points are important tips to remember as you run a business:

1. Back up your database regularly to prevent losing your data and to protect your investment in your database design. When you have a backup, you can always restore your entire database or selected database objects. If the number of records in your database grow too much, consider archiving older records.

2. Employ the right people, because if you can trust them, they can free you up to further develop your business properly.

3. Get a website. Your website is your presence on the Internet, allowing your customers, potential employees, business partners, and even investors to locate you and easily gather information about you and the products and services you offer.

4. If a customer gives you positive feedback, put it on your website. Feedback works like magic. It is a direct reflection of the services you offer, and when it's positive, it will help you build trust with your existing and potential customers.

5. Design eye-catching business cards to attract customers.

All the best, and may the Lord bless you in all the work of your hand, which you will do so that there shall not be room enough to receive it.

Frequently Asked Questions and Answers

1. What kind of business should I set up?

A. If the idea is yours and you initially want to work on your own, consider setting up as a sole trader.

B. If you want to work with someone else–if you want to share liabilities and responsibilities– then consider setting up as a partnership.

C. If you want to start the business with a huge amount of capital and run it as a director and receive a salary, or if you do not want to be personally liable to the activities of the business, then register as a limited company.

If you're still not sure which way to go, then see a professional advisor who will discuss which business status will be ideal for you.

2. How do I finance the business?

A. If you have spare cash, use it. Avoid borrowing in the initial stages. This will confirm to others that you are committed, and they will trust you more. However, make sure you keep some spare cash for emergencies, as you will be liable for the company's finances.

B. Check whether you qualify for a government or other grant for new starters or ongoing support in the form of training or even publicity. If you are eligible, the government will help you.

C. Take a business loan, a business overdraft, or even borrow from family and friends. Should you borrow from friends and family, make sure that everyone clearly agrees on the terms of repayment.

3. What do I need to know about taxes?

A. All types of businesses must pay taxes, be they sole traders, partnerships, or limited companies.

B. Check with the Inland Revenue to determine whether you need to pay taxes on capital gains. You may be liable for such taxes when you sell any assets of the company for profit.

4. What do I need to know about employing people?

A. Be very thorough in the recruitment process. Write a detailed job description, interview applicants, gather references, and make sure you choose the right person for the job.

B. Get legal advice about employment contracts. This will prevent legal and financial loss for your business.

C. Manage your staff fairly. Set clear expectations for both employees and yourself as the employer and follow all legal rules regarding hours, pay, leave entitlements, and so on.

5. How do I choose a business name?

A business name is the most immediate way to getting across the image you want your business to have, so your name needs to be memorable, and it should also work in different contexts–on your website, shopfront, your stationery, and everywhere else it appears.

You must also ensure that the name has not already been taken by someone else, especially one of your competitors. To do so, check online for the business name you have chosen or your local business registration office. You can also check in the Yellow Pages or Google the name.

It is also important that the name you choose does not limit your potential for growth. If the name reflects only a specific product or service, it might make it difficult to expand in the future.

6. **Do I need premises or may I work from home? If I need premises, what kind of premises do I need?**

   A. Starting a business from home has some advantages, including reduced expenses. However, working from home requires self-discipline, and dong so may also have insurance and legal implications.

   B. If you have the option to rent or buy a property for the business, carefully consider all the implications, especially the property's suitability for the type of business you wish to do. For example, are there enough parking spaces? Is there enough space to store your wares? The most important consideration of all is location. Will your existing and prospective customers be able to reach you easily?

7. **What legal issues do I need to be aware of?**

   A. Make sure your business complies with the latest legislation, including in employment law, contract law, health and safety regulations, and trading standards.

   B. Put all your business agreements in writing. This will prevent misunderstandings in the future. Contracts also help everybody understand their obligations from the onset.

C. If your business will be offering credit terms, make sure that the terms and conditions are provided with every sale.

APPENDIX 1

SAMPLE BUSINESS PLAN

Richco Weeding & Events Company Ltd.

1. Executive Summary

Richco, an event planning specialist, aims to bring a breath of fresh air into the event-planning market. By relying on old-fashioned values, going the extra mile, and using cutting-edge event-planning software, Richco will lead the market and provide quality results every time.

Richco is an equal opportunity business that makes its expertise and products available to help customers plan their own events. The event-planning software brings interactive event planning as close as customers' personal computers. Through these and other affordable products and services, Richco aims to be the number one resource for any event.

1.1 Company Objectives

Richco is a small business aimed at the big time. In order to reach its lofty goals, Richco intends to focus on the mission behind its vision. All employees, owners, founders, and vendors will live the vision of Richco daily. Richco will manifest this vision by:

- Being one of the top three event planning specialists in the UK.

- Justly compensating the employees, owners, and founders of Richco

- Producing the same quality results, every time.

1.2 Mission

In an ever changing fast-paced world, success is determined by good choices with lasting effects. Communication is essential. Richco strives to be the best choice for clients by helping to ease their event planning burdens. Through consistent, predictable professionalism, Richco will ensure a worry- and hassle-free event at a reasonable price.

Not all of our clients will be external to the business. Richco also has internal clients to serve. Richco will strive to provide the same predictable and professional working environment to all its employees, and it will justly compensate contracted vendors for their services. It is also a priority for Richco's owners, founders, full-time staff, and their families to make a comfortable living wage.

Keeping in tune with the needs of the market, utilising the latest technology and trends, all while ensuring clients receive the individual attention they deserve is the vision and daily mission of Richco.

1.3 Keys to Success

Our keys to success are the commitment to quality from every person who is part of the team. Each of us will be responsible for pushing ourselves to a higher level of professionalism in three areas:

1. Consistent, accurate fulfilment of the client's wishes.

2. Competitive pricing for the quality of services offered.

3. Significant profit made on each event planned.

2. Company Summary

Originally operated on a part-time basis, Richco is a small business designed to meet the needs of the ever changing social world. Kumasi is the current home, and plans are in place to expand to branch offices within four years. Richco's staff of two, along with numerous contract vendors, plans events, writes event-planning products, and trains area students in the art of event planning. Richco is invested in the community it resides in.

Richco is, in part, the answer to demands of the ever changing social world on the working family, heavily burdened office, out-of-town businessperson, or special person in need of special recognition. As a business, we understand the needs of public and private organisations. As parents and family members, we understand the needs of setting special time apart from other events in our lives. Richco strives to accomplish these goals in Kumasi and eventually in other areas of the Ashanti region.

2.1 Company Ownership

Richco is established as a sole proprietorship with the intention of selling the business when it is established to one of the employees invested in the vision of event planning. All aspects of the business's operations will be documented to ensure clients can count on the same results every time. It is these documents that will become the basis of ownership. The sole proprietor will use her name as the guarantor of each service. Therefore, the sole proprietor must embody the vision and mission of Richco.

2.2 Start-up Summary

Through careful planning on the part of the founders, the start-up costs for Richco are minimal. It began as a home-based business with little overhead, and it continues to demand fewer outlays of funds as a service-based business. The start-up investment funds were assets saved from prior earnings by the owners, who did event planning part time before establishing themselves as a business.

It is the wish of the founders to remain a debt-free establishment. However, recognising that, in reality, not all variables are controllable, outside financing is a viable option. Both founders own homes and have a perfect credit rating.

Start-up

Start-up Expenses

Legal	$200
Stationery, etc.	$300
Brochures	$185
Consultants	$200
Insurance	$145
Rent	$150
Expensed Equipment	$1,985
Other	$200
Total Start-up Expenses	$3,365

Start-up Assets	
Cash Required	$2,300
Start-up Inventory	$0
Other Current Assets	$0
Long-term Assets	$0
Total Assets	$2,300
Total Requirements	$5,665

Start-up Funding

Start-up Expenses to Fund	$3,365
Start-up Assets to Fund	$2,300
Total Funding Required	$5,665

Assets

Non-cash Assets from Start-up	$0
Cash Requirements from Start-up	$2,300
Additional Cash Raised	$0
Cash Balance on Starting Date	$2,300
Total Assets	$2,300

Liabilities and Capital

Liabilities

Current Borrowing	$2,000
Long-term Liabilities	$0
Accounts Payable (Outstanding Bills)	$0
Other Current Liabilities (Interest-free)	$0
Total Liabilities	$2,000

Capital

Planned Investment	
Sage Line 50	$3,400
Other	$265
Additional Investment Requirement	$0
Total Planned Investment	$3,665
Loss at Start-up (Start-up Expenses)	($3,365)
Total Capital	$300
Total Capital and Liabilities	$2,300
Total Funding	$5,665

2.3 Company Locations and Facilities

Richco is located inside the city limits of Kumasi. It is a home-based business. Most meetings with clients are conducted in social settings, such as at restaurants, coffee houses, the client's home, facilities to be used for the event, or over the phone. Although the demand has not yet reached its peak, Richco will eventually move from its home base into a small office complex, also within the city limits of Kumasi. When the company has reached its goals, Richco will have branch offices in Sunyani, Tamale, Konogo, and Accra.

The company will maintain a high degree of professionalism. All offices are equipped with the latest in business technology, including telephone systems, computers, fax machines, email accounts, duplicators, printers, and software. Each location will have a secure storage area for supplies and equipment used for events, such as walkie-talkies, cellular phones, portable fax machines, and laptops.

3. Products and Services

Although Richco is primarily a service business, we also offer products to aid our customers in planning events themselves. The following products are tools used inside our operation for the best possible results:

1. Party Pack

    The Party Pack is a complete kit for any party. It includes decorations, a lighting effects guide, themed disposable cameras, cutlery, plates, napkins, cups, punch mix, snack supplies, tablecloths, theme music, invitations, thank-you cards, and a step-by-step guide to planning, putting together, and hosting the event.

2. Step-by-Step Guides

    These booklets include a calendar to map out the event, a guide on what is needed for and how to put together a successful, worry-free event, resource information, popular refreshments with recipes, games, and tips to put the event in the record books. The events available include birthdays for all ages, meetings, retreats, parties, vacations, and special occasion celebrations such as graduations, holidays, showers, weddings, and receptions.

3. Event-Planning

Software Due to be released June 2000, this cutting-edge tool provides the client with all the resources and visual aids needed for their event planning. They will be able to play with decoration themes; listen to theme music; design invitations, thank-you cards, and RSVP cards; use the interactive planning calendar; and do much more. This software will bring their event into the millennium with cutting-edge technology that designed to save time and money.

4. Resources Manual

This valuable guide provides reviews for all event-planning resources located in the surrounding area. A ranking is given to the various services, including caterers, decorators, disc jockeys, bands, and facilities. This manual gives the client the freedom to make a choice based on experience.

5. Free Event Planners Training for High School and College Students

   As a member of the Portland community, it is our mission to support our community. Ten hours each month will be devoted to training area students in event planning. This will aid them in planning proms, graduation parties, river clean-ups, homecoming, and other important events. This is a priority of Richco. It will not be cut back as the business grows.

Richco provides event planning in a wide range of applications. We guarantee satisfaction in the areas of appearance, performance, and taste. The following is a sampling of the types of events we plan every year:

1. Corporate meetings, training programmes, and retreats.

2. Conferences and workshops.

3. Birthdays, anniversaries, graduations, and holidays.

4. Weddings, receptions, and showers.

5. Company picnics, banquets, and award ceremonies.

3.1 Competitive Comparison

Richco, although young, draws from the age-old tradition of going above and beyond what is expected, every time. Our systems for event planning have been drawn up, evaluated, practiced, worked, and reworked to ensure maximum efficiency while minimising the possibility for error. We employ local vendors who have the same desire to be the best at what they do while providing un-matchable services. Thus, we give back to the community by providing jobs outside of our organisation. We encourage new and upcoming small businesses who provide a service within our need base to step up to the challenge of being the best through their contract with Richco.

Our products will serve the function of aiding those that cannot afford the cost of an event planner. We wish to make our event planning tips available to those who need a helping hand. Richco is a member of the community. Through event planning, Richco gets the opportunity to laugh when the community laughs and cry when the community cries, to rejoice when the community rejoices and to help put the pieces back together when things fall apart. We care about the things that have meaning in the lives of our neighbours.

4. Market Analysis Summary

The following sections describe the market segmentation, strategy, and industry analyses.

4.1 Market Segmentation

The market for event planning constitutes a wide, very diverse group. Individuals as well as organisations demand the services we provide. In order to provide the greatest depth of information, the market segments have been broken down into private and public organisations, and age groups.

1. Private Organisations and Businesses

   Private organisations make up the single largest portion of Richco's client base. Private organisations such as businesses, corporations, and political parties host the most events on the largest scales; therefore, these events generate larger revenues per event. The majority of larger scale holiday functions will fall under this segment.

2. Public Organisations

   Government agencies host many events every year. Richco hopes to alleviate the pressure of event planning for public employees. The second single largest segment, the public sector, can save money and give back to its community at the same time. These events are moderate in scale with middle to low revenues generated. Emphasis is placed on the visibility of the event for public viewing. The majority of organisational family functions will fall under this segment.

3. Age Breakdowns

o Under 24: Persons under the age of twenty-four using an event planner are rare at best. We hope to tap the early college graduates who have begun their professional careers but have not yet started their families. These events will focus mainly on themes with moderate to high energy appeal. The revenues generated will range from moderate to high, depending on the event. The majority of weddings will fall into this segment.

o Ages 25-55: The persons that fall into this age group are employed, middle- to upper-middle-class families. The reason they choose event planners is they are too busy to do it themselves. Therefore, Richco will be on hand to answer questions, and contact will be moderate in length but will occur regularly so as not to disturb the daily life of the families. These events will generate moderate revenues, with a few generating low revenues. The majority of special occasion planning will occur in this market segment.

o Ages 56 and above: Persons over the age of fifty-five have reached the turning point of life. Many are retiring, others are celebrating anniversaries of significant years, and still others are seeing that their children's special events are taken care of. These events will generate moderate to high revenues depending upon the income level of the family. Most holiday parties and other special occasions such as wedding receptions and reunions will occur in this market segment.

4. Other

This segment has no direct information to compile for a description. It consists of any event planned that does not fit into one of the above categories.

Market Analysis (Pie)

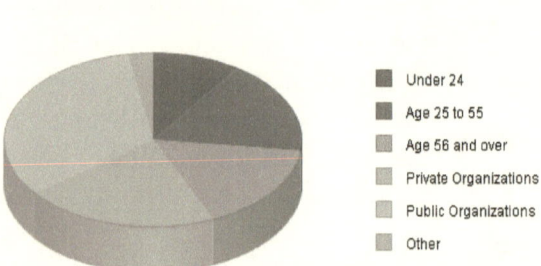

- Under 24
- Age 25 to 55
- Age 56 and over
- Private Organizations
- Public Organizations
- Other

Market Analysis

		Year 1	Year 2	Year 3	Year 4	Year 5	
Potential Customers	Growth						CAGR
Under 24	0%	18	18	20	21	22	5.14%
Age 25 to 55	0%	33	33	44	51	59	15.63%
Age 56 and over	0%	31	31	37	40	44	9.15%
Private Organisations	0%	40	40	102	163	261	59.83%
Public Organisations	0%	62	62	105	137	178	30.17%
Other	0%	5	5	7	8	9	15.83%
Total	31.95%	189	189	315	420	573	31.95%

4.2 Target Market Segment Strategy

Our target markets are middle- to upper-middle-class families, couples, and individuals and private and public organisations. We chose these groups because they are most able to afford event planners and have the least amount of time to spare for event planning in general. Families demand attention, employees are overburdened, and overwhelming detail needed to plan large events are too large a constraint to place on people not trained in the area of event planning.

The fast pace of the world we live in leaves little time for extra things we would like to do, like plan events, parties, and social get-togethers. Richco fills the need by being available to take on the burden of planning so that people can spend time on more important things like family and friends. The demand for this service can only increase considering the rise in incomes, population, and need for interpersonal relations in the workplace.

4.3 Service Business Analysis

Richco is in a unique position of competition. We compete against hotels with conference facilities, conference centres, other event planners both on the large and small scale, persons within an organisation who are assigned the task of organising an event, and people who wish to organise their own events without the benefit of assistance. The benefits and of each of our competitors as compared with the services we offer are hardly a match in quality and price.

1. **Hotels and Conference Centres**

   Strengths: On-site facilities, equipment, and support staff; ability to transport and house persons for overnight stays; able to internalise costs of transportation and equipment. **Weaknesses:** Often very expensive and impersonal. They rely on unskilled labour for support staff. The error rate is high due to high volume and traffic from other events happening at the same time.

2. **Other Event Planners**

   Strengths: Have been in the market longer, have established a reputation and client base. **Weaknesses:** Reputation precedes them, no systems-based businesses designed to produce consistent results; focus on smaller events and specialised events rather than all events; do not have the supporting products to market with, or instead of, event planning services.

3. Employees or Persons Wishing to Do It Themselves

Strengths: Internalised cost of planning the event; able to add tiny personalised touches that have meaning within the group or family. **Weaknesses:** Prefer to spend time on other things; don't have access to the best prices, services, and other needed resources.

5. Strategy and Implementation Summary

We have discussed our client base as being predominately middle- to upper-middle-class individuals, couples, and families and public and private organisations. We must then look at the needs of these markets and cater to them. We promise the same great results, every time.

When marketing to individuals, the idea of releasing them from the task, freeing their time for family and friends, and the promise of a worry-free event are the buzzwords and key concepts. Our marketing is predominantly by word of mouth or visual connection to large events these individuals have participated in or worked at.

When marketing to public or private organisations, the idea of greater efficiency for the money and a professional event without error is the key concept.

Groups, especially large ones, do not wish to deal with problems that arise due to oversight on their part. If the guarantee of worry-free, error-free events is available at a cost benefit to them, there really appears to be no better choice.

5.1 Sales Strategy

Richco deals with a diverse market of clients. Within each market segment, sales closings will differ. Each approach is described as follows:

1. **Private and Public Organisations**

   Sales will be concluded one to two days after the end of the event. A follow-up phone call will be placed informing the client of the total cost, number of attendees, and information about the billing packet that will arrive at their offices. Feedback forms will be included in these packets to ensure the client is being served as they deem appropriate. Form thank-you letter will be sent following each event.

2. **Individuals**

   Sales will be concluded with a follow-up phone call one to two days after the event. The phone call will explain the total cost of the event, number of attendees, and information concerning the billing. Individual parties of any age group are placed on a billing cycle.

Invoices will be sent out the 25th of the month and will be due the 10th of the following month. Feedback forms will be included in these packets to ensure the client is being served as they deem appropriate. Thank-you cards will follow each individual event.

5.1.1 Sales Forecast

By beginning on a smaller scale, Richco has the foresight to grow at a rapid pace to keep up with demand. We wish to maintain a steady rate of sales growth; however, we understand that sales of products and services will vary in different months. As noted in the table, rapid increases during the holiday season will boost sales, and then allow that growth to level off at a steady rate.

Sales Forecast

	Year 1	Year 2	Year 3
Sales			
Private	$206,170	$276,099	$299,002
Public	$113,185	$178,490	$193,000
Other	$33,794	$40,081	$62,777
Total Sales	**$353,149**	**$494,670**	**$554,779**
Direct Cost of Sales	**Year 1**	**Year 2**	**Year 3**
Private	$28,864	$38,654	$41,860
Public	$11,319	$17,849	$19,300
Other	$1,690	$2,004	$3,139
Total Direct Cost of Sales	**$41,872**	**$58,507**	**$64,299**

5.2 Milestones

The milestones chart shows specific detail about actual programme activities that should be taking place during the year. Each one has its manager, starting date, ending date, and budget. During the year, we will be keeping track of implementation against the plan, with reports on the timely completion of these activities as planned.

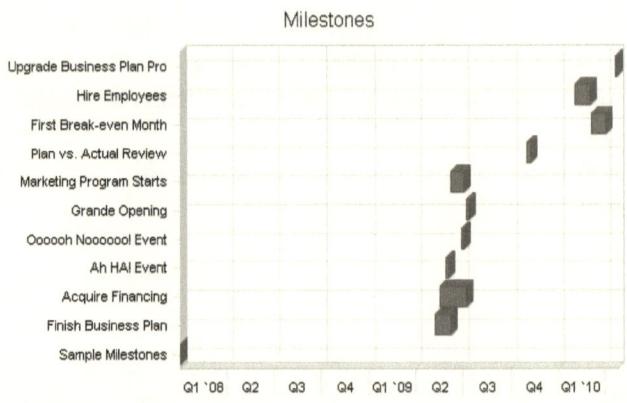

6. Management Summary

Information and expense details are presented in "Organisational Structure" and "Personnel Plan" below.

6.1 Organisational Structure

The management team within Richco will be small in the beginning. The primary employee is the founder, who plans events, then contracts with caterers, decorators, disc jockeys, and bands to fill out the event. A contract-labour site manager will be on hand to work the events as a liaison and vendor coordinator. Thus, there are two main employees with various of vendors.

When Richco reaches its expansion goals, each office will have one to two event planners, an office assistant, two to three site managers for the events, and a product and marketing specialist. This team will function as one with constant communication through weekly staff meetings, email, and message boards. All jobs are interrelated. The performance of one effects the performance of the others; therefore, each team member expects nothing but the best from each other.

As it functions currently, we see no gaps in the management of this organisation. Should Richco grow beyond its estimated size, more positions in specialised areas will need to be added as well as additional site support and office assistance. To fill these positions, Richco is looking for energetic, teachable, detail-oriented people who want the potential to grow and improve their skills within the organisation. Richco wants to be the best; therefore, we will hire those who want to succeed.

6.2 Personnel Plan

The following table shows the estimated personnel needs for Richco.

Personnel Plan

	Year 1	Year 2	Year 3
Event Specialist	$36,000	$40,000	$42,000
Site Manager	$11,097	$13,750	$14,560
Other	$8,947	$9,560	$10,000
Total People	0	0	0
Total Payroll	$56,044	$63,310	$66,560

7. Financial Plan

Service-based businesses require few funds to start up, and as they grow and expand, fewer funds to maintain. The charts and graphs that follow will show that investment up front allows Richco to function debt-free with little overhead. This gives Richco a quicker break-even point and increased profit margins from the start. As Richco grows, the debt-free philosophy will be maintained until it is impossible to function during growth periods without financial assistance.

7.1 Important Assumptions

Tax rates are noted for information. We carry no loan burden that would be affected by these rates. What hits Richco the hardest (but not nearly as hard as other service businesses), is the tax rate of 24%, which is nearly one-quarter of total sales. As Richco continues to grow, these numbers will be reference rather than influence.

General Assumptions

	Year 1	Year 2	Year 3
Plan Month	1	2	3
Current Interest Rate	10.00%	10.00%	10.00%
Long-term Interest Rate	10.00%	10.00%	10.00%
Tax Rate	24.00%	24.00%	24.00%
Other	0	0	0

7.2 Key Financial Indicators

The break-even point for Richco is based on the assumption that we will produce 22 events per month and average approximately $521 per event. In the current situation, we average more than this assumption for our public- and private-organisation events. These currently make up 18 of the 22 events hosted per month on average.

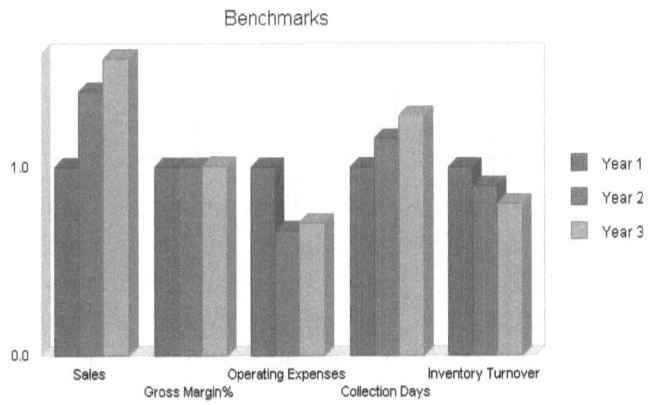

7.3 Break-even Analysis

The break-even point will appear more rapidly for Richco than for other types of home-based businesses. Start-up costs are limited to minimal equipment, there is little or no staff to pay in the beginning, and contracted companies will handle any additional equipment required for the planned events.

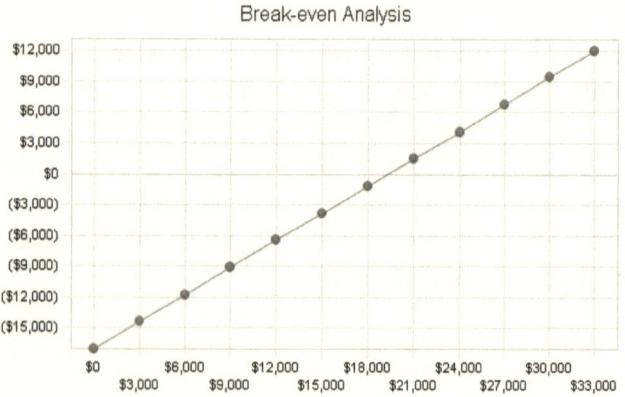

7.4 Projected Profit and Loss

Leading the industry in event planning requires the use of the resources available at the lowest cost. As noted in the table below, we spend less money on overhead than other event planners with an outside office or office space in their own facility. This savings allows us to market in creative ways and spend funds on expansion into other areas when the time is right.

Pro Forma Profit and Loss

	Year 1	Year 2	Year 3
Sales	$353,149	$494,670	$554,779
Direct Cost of Sales	$41,872	$58,507	$64,299
Other Costs of Sales	$196	$203	$221
Total Cost of Sales	$42,068	$58,710	$64,520
Gross Margin	$311,081	$435,960	$490,259
Gross Margin %	88.09%	88.13%	88.37%
Expenses			
Payroll	$56,044	$63,310	$66,560
Sales & Marketing & Other Expenses	$146,013	$68,400	$73,400
Depreciation	$0	$0	$0
Leased Equipment	$0	$0	$0
Utilities	$516	$750	$800
Insurance	$264	$750	$1,000
Rent	$1,440	$1,800	$1,800
Payroll Taxes	$0	$0	$0
Other	$0	$0	$0
Total Operating Expenses	$204,277	$135,010	$143,560
Profit Before Interest and Taxes	$106,804	$300,950	$346,699
EBITDA	$106,804	$300,950	$346,699
Interest Expense	$406	$279	$362
Taxes Incurred	$25,535	$72,161	$83,121
Net Profit	$80,862	$228,510	$263,216
Net Profit/Sales Ratio	22.90%	46.19%	47.45%

7.5 Projected Cash Flow

Our cash situation is solid. Although we begin with little extra cash, our increased growth allows us to make up for lost time. Our cash balance is always above the mark with the cash flow not too far behind. We have no negatives in our cash analysis.

Pro Forma Cash Flow

	Year 1	Year 2	Year 3
Cash Received			
Cash from Operations			
Cash Sales	$141,260	$197,868	$221,912
Cash from Receivables	$178,271	$283,330	$327,145
Subtotal Cash from Operations	**$319,531**	**$481,198**	**$549,057**
Additional Cash Received			
Sales Tax, VAT, HST/GST Received	$0	$0	$0
New Current Borrowing	$4,000	$1,080	$1,080
New Other Liabilities (interest-free)	$0	$0	$0
New Long-term Liabilities	$0	$0	$0
Sales of Other Current Assets	$0	$0	$0
Sales of Long-term Assets	$0	$0	$0
New Investment Received	$0	$0	$0
Subtotal Cash Received	**$323,531**	**$482,278**	**$550,137**
Expenditures	Year 1	Year 2	Year 3
Expenditures from Operations			
Cash Spending	$56,044	$63,310	$66,560
Bill Payments	$199,964	$209,268	$223,979

Subtotal Spent on Operations	$256,008	$272,578	$290,539
Additional Cash Spent			
Sales Tax, VAT, HST/GST Paid Out	$0	$0	$0
Principal Repayment of Current Borrowing	$3,500	$500	$0
Other Liabilities Principal Repayment	$0	$0	$0
Long-term Liabilities Principal Repayment	$0	$0	$0
Purchase Other Current Assets	$0	$0	$0
Purchase Long-term Assets	$0	$0	$0
Dividends	$0	$0	$0
Subtotal Cash Spent	$259,508	$273,078	$290,539
Net Cash Flow	$64,023	$209,200	$259,598
Cash Balance	$66,323	$275,523	$535,121

7.6 Projected Balance Sheet

Richco is set up for success. According to the numbers, we start out fair and end up amazing. By FY2000, we will be worth over $125,000 with a profit margin of over 30%. We are operating with little to zero debt, boosting the net worth even higher. Our only weakness is that the products to be released in FY2000 have not been accounted for as an investment of funds. This will affect the cash flow in a moderate way, and it is undetermined how it will affect the profit ratio of the business.

Pro Forma Balance Sheet

	Year 1	Year 2	Year 3
Assets			
Current Assets			
Cash	$66,323	$275,523	$535,121
Accounts Receivable	$33,618	$47,090	$52,812
Inventory	$4,991	$6,975	$7,665
Other Current Assets	$0	$0	$0
Total Current Assets	*$104,933*	*$329,588*	*$595,598*
Long-term Assets			
Long-term Assets	$0	$0	$0
Accumulated Depreciation	$0	$0	$0
Total Long-term Assets	$0	$0	$0
Total Assets	*$104,933*	*$329,588*	*$595,598*

Liabilities and Capital	**Year 1**	**Year 2**	**Year 3**
Current Liabilities			
Accounts Payable	$21,270	$16,836	$18,550
Current Borrowing	$2,500	$3,080	$4,160
Other Current Liabilities	$0	$0	$0
Subtotal Current Liabilities	*$23,770*	*$19,916*	*$22,710*
Long-term Liabilities	$0	$0	$0
Total Liabilities	$23,770	$19,916	$22,710

Paid-in Capital	$3,665	$3,665	$3,665
Retained Earnings	($3,365)	$77,497	$306,007
Earnings	$80,862	$228,510	$263,216
Total Capital	$81,162	$309,672	$572,888
Total Liabilities and Capital	***$104,933***	***$329,588***	***$595,598***
Net Worth	**$81,162**	**$309,672**	**$572,888**

APPENDIX 2

HOW TO PREPARE AN INVOICE

Your business needs to raise invoices for the services you provide. Include the following information on all invoices:

Company Details

Include the following information about your business:

❖ Company name

❖ Company address

❖ Company telephone number and email address

❖ Company number

❖ VAT registration number (if VAT registered)

Invoice Number

Each of your invoices should have a unique invoice number, and although this is called a *number*, it can include letters. A common method is to prefix invoices with letters that indicate the client.

For example: If you provided services for GPL and FLSC, for GPL, you could use GPL001, GPL002, and so on. For FLSC, you could use FLSC001, FLSC002, and so on.

Dates

Include the following dates:

- ❖ The date the invoice was raised.

- ❖ The date by which payment should be made. This is most often 30 days after the invoice date, but the terms will vary according to your agreements with customers.

Client details

Provide the name and address of the agency or client being billed.

Fees

This section requires the following:

- ❖ A description of the services provided

- ❖ The gross amount due

- ❖ The VAT amount, if you are VAT registered

- ❖ The total amount due

For example:

20 Days @ £500 per day	Amount:	£10,000
	VAT:	£2,000
	Total:	£12,000

Payment terms:

Specify by what method you would like to receive the money. For example: "Payment should be made within 30 days by cheque or money transfer."